CHEETAHS

Cheetah Magic for Kids

METRIC CONVERSIONS:

1 mile = 1.609 kilometers
1 pound = .4536 kilogram

To my grandchildren, Marlon and Melodie
—Winnie MacPherson

For a free color catalog describing Gareth Stevens Publishing's list of high-quality books and multimedia programs, call 1-800-542-2595 (USA) or 1-800-461-9120 (Canada). Gareth Stevens Publishing's Fax: 414-225-0377.

Library of Congress Cataloging-in-Publication Data

MacPherson, Winnie, 1930-
    Cheetah magic for kids / by Winnie MacPherson; illustrated by
John F. McGee.
        p. cm. (Animal magic for kids)
    "Based on the book, Cheetahs for kids . . . by Winnie MacPherson" —
T.p. verso.
    Includes bibliographical references and index.
    Summary: Describes the physical characteristics, habitat, and behavior
of this swift African cat through the viewpoint of Beth, an eleven-year-old
daughter of wildlife photographers.
    ISBN 0-8368-2631-0 (lib. bdg.)
    1. Cheetah—Juvenile literature. [1. Cheetah.] I. McGee, John F., ill.
II. Title. III. Series.
QL737.C23M2235   2000
599.75'9—dc21   99-053512

First published in this edition in
North America in 2000 by
Gareth Stevens Publishing
1555 North RiverCenter Drive, Suite 201
Milwaukee, WI 53212 USA

Based on the book, *Cheetahs for Kids*, text © 1998 by Winnie MacPherson, with illustrations by John F. McGee. First published in the United States in 1998 by NorthWord Press, Inc., (Creative Publishing International), 5900 Green Oak Drive, Minnetonka, MN 55343. End matter © 2000 by Gareth Stevens, Inc.

Photographs © 1998: Stephen J. Krasemann: cover; Erwin and Peggy Bauer: 3, 26, 38-39, back cover; Craig Brandt: 7; Dembinsky Photo Associates: Fritz Polking: 8, 13, 22, 24-25, 30, 34, 40; Adam Jones: 14; Mike Barlow: 42; Mark J. Thomas: 47; Len Rue, Jr.: 10-11, 28-29; Art Wolfe: 16, 18-19, 21.

Printed in the United States of America

1 2 3 4 5 6 7 8 9 04 03 02 01 00

by Winnie MacPherson

CHEETAHS

Cheetah Magic for Kids

Gareth Stevens Publishing
MILWAUKEE

AFRICA

Serengeti

After traveling many miles on trains, boats and airplanes, we finally arrived in Africa. My name is Beth and I am 11 years old. My parents are wildlife photographers. We are always visiting interesting and exciting places so they can take pictures.

For the first time, we were on the plains of the Serengeti in Africa, to photograph cheetahs. The Serengeti is a wildlife refuge covering thousands of square miles in eastern Africa.

Cheetahs live on this open grassland, where they find their favorite prey such as gazelles and impalas. Sometimes, they also hunt hares. Those animals live here because they like to eat the grass and small plants that grow here on the Serengeti.

On the first day of our trip, I awoke before dawn. I was much too excited to fall back asleep. It was time to get up if I was going to see some cheetahs. They usually hunt early in the morning before the sun is too hot.

After breakfast, I helped my dad put the cameras in the truck. Our guide knew a lot about cheetahs and took us to places where they could be observed. Using my binoculars, I saw many unusual animals. I couldn't wait to see a real cheetah!

As we rode along, I thought about some of the things I knew about cheetahs. They belong to the cat family, whose members are called felids (FE-lidz).

Cheetah cubs stay near their mother for protection.

Cheetahs often climb trees to play, to look around and to leave scent marks. But cheetahs never climb trees to hide their prey in the branches, as leopards do. Cheetahs outrun their prey on the open plains, instead of pouncing on it from a hiding place, as lions and leopards do.

Cheetahs may seem to be flying as they chase their prey.

Like most cats, however, cheetahs are solitary animals. This means they live and hunt alone. Once a year the male and female come together to mate. But they do not stay together. Each goes its own way. The mother must feed and protect her young babies by herself.

Cheetahs are the star sprinters of the cat family. They would win a race with any of their relatives, even the larger cats like lions and tigers. Cheetahs are the fastest animals on land, often reaching speeds of 70 miles per hour.

Pages 10-11: Cheetahs like to climb up on things in order to see farther.

FINISH

9

We had driven about 20 minutes when, suddenly, I saw a family of cheetahs. A female cheetah was sitting on top of a large termite mound. Her three young, called cubs, were sitting with her.

Cheetahs like to sit on the high mounds so they can watch what is going on around them. It is a good way to look for prey and for enemies.

When we drove closer, the mother came down from the top of the mound and stood watching us. Cheetahs are really shy animals. This mother was cautious about anything coming too close to her cubs.

Cubs must learn to be still and watchful.

The mother was beautiful. She was standing tall and proud. Her short, golden fur was covered with black spots. In fact, the name cheetah means "spotted one." The spots on her tail made rings toward the fluffy tip, which was white. Her belly was also white.

Because she had such a large chest and large thigh muscles, her waist looked extra small. She had long, thin legs. They looked very strong. Her feet were thin too, not rounded like other cats' feet.

Her head was rounded on top and seemed very small. Cheetahs have a brow that sticks out over their sharp-sighted eyes. This helps protect their eyes from the sun. In very bright light, the pupils of their golden eyes become small dots.

The Serengeti grasses are good camouflage.

Like other members of the cat family, cheetahs have excellent eyesight.

Two black stripes ran down the female's face. They started from the inner corner of each eye and went around the outside of her mouth. Some scientists call these stripes "tear lines," since they run down a cheetah's face like tears. These lines and their spots are good camouflage (KAM-uh-flaj) for the cheetah when it hides in the grass. They help cheetahs get very close to prey without being seen.

The female's small, round ears were low on her head. Her hearing is so keen she may hear prey before she sees it. And when she hears a sound, she doesn't have to turn her head as humans do to find out where it came from. She just moves her ears.

The cubs had the same color and markings as their mother—except that their bodies were covered with a layer of long, smoke-gray fur. It was like the fluff on a baby bird. This fur was even longer on their shoulders and down their back.

They will lose this gray fur when they are about 3 months old. Then their coat will be golden like their mother's.

Cubs don't hurt each other when they play-fight.

19

We guessed that the cubs were about 6 weeks old. During the first six weeks of their life, cubs stay in their lair under a bush. The female cheetah has to leave them alone when she goes hunting.

This might have been the cubs' first day out on the plains with their mother. These cheetah cubs were born before the spring rainy season had turned the grass green. I could see that their baby fur blended with the dry grass. It helped to hide the cubs.

The female had brought the cubs with her so they would be closer to their food. Before she could hunt, though, she had to find a new safe lair where the cubs could rest.

As the fluffy cub grows, its fur will become sleek.

The cubs would not be able to help their mother hunt yet. In fact, they might make trouble for her. Such young cubs often accidentally warn the prey with their whimpering and playing in the grass. From 6 to 12 months old, the cubs follow their mother to learn her skills when she hunts. They will not hunt large prey on their own until they are about 12 to 16 months old.

Sometimes cubs want to play when they should be learning to hunt.

The largest of the cubs became curious and slowly moved down from the mound. It stood near its mother and stared at me. Suddenly, the cub wrinkled its face and spat.

This startled me and made me jump. But I couldn't help laughing. The cub was so small, and it tried so hard to be ferocious.

Soon the female decided that we were not going to harm them. She made a chirping sound, and the other two cubs came to her.

The cheetah family slowly moved away from us across the plains. The female cheetah's sharp eyes kept watching for prey to catch for dinner. She must hunt every day to feed herself and her cubs. Cheetahs can live for 5 or more days without water, if they have meat to eat.

Newborn cheetahs get all their food from their mother.

Shade from a tree is a good place for a cheetah to rest.

We followed them while Mom and Dad took pictures. Finally, they turned and disappeared into the tall grass. All we could see was the white tip of the female's tail. It is this white tip of their mother's tail that the cubs follow when going through high grass. I watched it too, until they were out of sight.

The hot sun was burning my face. We decided it was time to return to our camp and the shade of the trees. The cheetahs were leaving the open plains for the shelter of their bushes.

The next day, we returned to the same place, hoping to see the female with her cubs again. A hot wind blew across the plains.

On our way, we passed some young male cheetahs roaming across the grass together. Sometimes, after leaving their mother, young cheetah brothers live and hunt together. These groups of young males are called coalitions (ko-uh-LISH-unz). They hunt and protect their small territory of about 15 square miles.

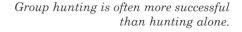

Group hunting is often more successful than hunting alone.

All at once we saw a female cheetah. She was growling, and she kept looking nervously at a nearby large clump of bushes.

Suddenly we saw four female lions running toward the bush.

"I know what's worrying her," Dad said. "She has cubs hidden in the bush. If the lions find her cubs, they will kill them. The cheetah cannot go near the bush or she will reveal the cubs' hiding place."

It was clear the lions were searching for something. I was sure they had scented (SENT-ed), or smelled, the cheetah cubs. Then I realized they weren't even looking at the bush. They ran right past it. The cubs were safe!

Cubs must stay alert when they are hiding from danger.

As soon as the lions were gone, the female cheetah ran to the bush and called her cubs to her. She used the same chirping sound we had heard the day before.

Cheetahs also make many other sounds like squeals, yelps and purrs. Some are used for teaching the cubs. Some are used for warning of danger. Some are used when they are contented.

Females often purr loudly while washing or feeding their cubs. Male cheetahs, however, do not roar, as lions do.

PURR-R-R-R

Mother cheetahs are very patient with their playful cubs.

On the tenth day of our trip, we found our cheetah family again. The female was sitting on the same termite mound. One of the cubs was sitting between her front legs. I saw the other two playing at the bottom of the mound.

One cub hid in the grass and leaped out at the other when it passed. Then they rolled together in the grass, over and over. They took turns hiding and pouncing.

Sometimes they gave each other little nips on the back or neck. When cubs run and play-fight they are really practicing for when they grow up and have to hunt and defend themselves.

Soon the mother cheetah and the third cub joined in the game of hide-and-pounce. She was enjoying the game as much as the cubs. It was fun watching them play.

At one time, all four of the cheetahs were chasing each other in a circle. The mother and cubs played together for quite a while. She was very patient, even when they tugged on her tail and jumped at her face.

Suddenly, the female stopped and began watching a nearby herd of impalas eating leaves from bushes. The impalas did not see the cheetahs. Giving her cubs the signal to hide, she slowly crouched low to the ground. The cubs ran under a bush.

Silently, the mother cheetah moved through the thin grass toward the impalas. She never stopped watching them. If she felt the impalas had seen her, she crouched and stayed perfectly still.

Her sneaky walk quickened to a run. Suddenly, she was in a super sprint!

Cheetahs have good balance, even when running at top speed.

The dry dust from the plains flew up in a cloud behind her. When the impalas saw the cheetah racing toward them, they rushed away in a stampede.

Impalas keep an eye on nearby cheetahs at all times.

Cheetahs are built for running at high speed. Everything about them is light and sleek. In fact, an adult cheetah only weighs about 100 to 130 pounds. Some lions weigh as much as 500 pounds.

Cheetahs have slender bodies and small heads. Their narrow, sharp teeth fit together in their jaw, and work like scissor blades. There is no space for the large front teeth other cats have.

Their whiskers are short and not very thick. Since they hunt in the grass during the day, they don't need long whiskers to help them find their way through thick, dark bushes.

The claws on a cheetah's small, thin feet are not retractable like those of a house cat. This means they cannot be pulled back into their toes. Because the claws are out all the time, they lose their sharpness and become worn down. But this wearing down makes them thick and strong.

A big yawn shows the cheetah's sharp teeth.

The pads on a cheetah's feet are small and tough. When the cheetah runs, the edges of the pads grip the ground like rubber soles on sneakers. Cheetahs also have strong leg muscles.

The cheetah's limber spine is another key to its speed. It works like a spring. The cheetah curves its back and pulls its feet together. Then, the back uncoils and the long legs fly out as far as they can reach. As soon as the front legs touch the ground again, the spine coils up and gives the legs another powerful push.

Each time the cheetah's back bends and stretches, it gives more power to the legs to reach even farther. The cheetah soars through the air in mighty leaps!

A cheetah's strong feet and short, tough claws tightly grip the ground. Its long, thick tail swings back and forth as the cheetah turns and twists after its prey. The tail helps to keep the cheetah balanced.

While on a chase, the cheetah breathes in huge gulps of air through large nostrils to its large lungs. It may take as many as 150 breaths a minute. This is much faster than its regular breathing.

From standing still, cheetahs can reach a speed of 70 miles per hour in seconds. But cheetahs must catch their prey very quickly, for they cannot continue this high speed for much longer than a minute or two.

As we watched, a few of the impalas waited too long before running away, and they were left behind. The female cheetah caught one of them. At last, she had food for her cubs and herself.

Cheetahs must protect their kill from other predators.

But she could not eat yet. Her powerful race had used up all the strength in her body. And she was overheated. She lay down to rest and cool off.

While the cheetah rests, other predators may come and steal the prey. Hyenas, lions and jackals all steal from cheetahs. So the cheetah must try to hide her prey and rest quickly. She must be very lucky. Any of those predators might also kill the cheetah's cubs.

After about 15 minutes, she had caught her breath. Her heart had slowed to its normal beating. The mother cheetah returned to the cubs' hiding place and showed the cubs the way back to the kill. Finally, the cheetah family was able to eat.

A few days later, we had to leave. My parents had taken all the pictures they needed. I was sad that it was time to end our stay on the Serengeti. I would miss our cheetah family.

Maybe I would see the cheetahs on another visit. I was sure I would never forget them.

GLOSSARY

Camouflage: The color and markings of some animals that help the animals blend in with their surroundings (pages 15, 16).

Felid: The family name for cats, such as cheetahs, lions, tigers, jaguars, and wild and domestic cats (page 6).

Lair: The resting or living place of a wild animal (page 20).

Predators: Animals that hunt other animals for food (pages 45, 46).

Prey: Animals that are hunted by other animals for food (pages 5, 8, 12, 16, 17, 22, 24, 44, 45, 46).

Retractable: Having the ability to withdraw or take back in (page 42).

Sprinters / sprint: Very fast runners/a very fast run (pages 9, 38).

Stampede: A sudden rushing or flight of frightened animals (page 40).

Territory: An area of land occupied and defended by an animal or group of animals (page 28).

MORE BOOKS TO READ

Big Cats. Animal Families (series) by Markus Kappeler (Gareth Stevens)

Cheetahs. Nature Watch (series) by Dianne M. MacMillan (Carolrhoda)

Cheetahs: Fleetest of Foot. Secrets of the Animal World (series) by Eulalia García (Gareth Stevens)

Swift as the Wind: The Cheetah by Barbara J. Esbensen (Orchard)

VIDEOS

The Cheetah's Tale (Library Video)

Cheetahs with Holly Hunter (PBS Home Video)

Cheetahs: The Winning Streak (Library Video)

WEB SITES

www.cheetahspot.com

www.primenet.com/~brendel/cheet.html

Some web sites stay current longer than others. For further web sites, use your search engines to locate the following topics: *camouflage, cats, cheetahs, felids, Serengeti,* and *wildlife in Africa.*